HOPE FOR WOMEN IN TRIAL

EMBRACING ALL SEASONS OF LIFE

By
(Je Taun Barron)

Ebook ISBN: 979-8-9876066-1-2
Paperback ISBN: 979-8-9876066-0-5

This book is dedicated to my dad David C. Verdun.

Thank you for your love, your patience, the sacrifices you made, and your support.

You were well-loved everywhere you served. Thank you for community.

As you look down from heaven, I hope you're proud of the woman that I have become.

Enjoy your Ferrari!

To my devoted husband Cosmo thank you for beliving in me, understanding me, loving me unconditionally and encouraging me to follow my dreams.
I love you!

To my mom and sister: thank you for dedicated support and prayers.

To every woman who needs hope and encouragement: this is for you.

I pray this book blesses you abundantly.

Table of Contents

INTRODUCTION

Women are co-bearers of God's image (Genesis 1:27). They share this image with men, even though God made them differently. Eve, whom God created from Adam's rib, was exquisitely designed to complete and complement him. She was given to Adam by God. "In the end! This one is made out of bone and flesh. She will be referred to as a 'woman' since she was taken from a 'man.'" Adam made these remarks about the woman in Genesis 2:23 (NLT).

As the nurturers of humanity and mothers of procreation, women are unique beings. Despite what some people may believe, women are not weaker than men. In fact, the pain women experience every month and the suffering they endure during nine months of pregnancy are testaments to their strength, challenging the idea they are weaker vessels. I could go on and on about women and the indisputable qualities that make them special.

Women's lives can be very difficult, especially if they live alone and have no one to share their suffering with or to recognize their efforts.

If you are a woman or young girl reading this book, I want you to know I am sympathetic to your suffering and wish to help ease the burdens you are carrying. But ultimately, everything will be fine. Truth is with every new season comes change and occasionally unpleasant difficulties. It's normal to feel exhausted, trip, bend to your limits, and go limp from strain.

Life can be challenging when it seems no one is interested in you. You might struggle with dark thoughts and wish the suffering would end permanently. However, let me remind you that while pain may be a part of the process, it's not your final destination. It's temporary. God knows you, cares about you, and loves you very much. His love for you is unconditional. Even in your darkest hour, remember better times are coming, and they are not far off. God is your Creator, and nothing is hidden from His sight. He knew you before you were even conceived in your mother's womb.

Joy and sorrow coexist in life; they are both present. So you might occasionally encounter swells of sorrow, deep sorrows, and additional life challenges that leave you wondering how you'll get through another day. But you are not alone. God is with you every step of the way He is aware of your situation, and He is taking action.

If you're going through a challenging time and it feels as if the end is near, cling to God. Don't give up. There is hope, even during the most terrible times of your life when everything is bare, and all seems lost.

A tiny glimmer of hope can have a significant impact. Hope and fortitude enable us to set goals, persevere through hardships, and thrive. God is always with you, regardless of what you are going through. Sometimes in life, it seems as though the people around you are having an easier time than you are, and your life is going in a different direction. Remember that God made us for specific missions and extraordinary journeys; therefore, whatever is happening in your life is not happening to you but for you.

Never lose sight of the reality that each season has a specific goal. Your journey, struggles, and the puzzling riddles with solutions that deftly elude you whenever you get close all have a purpose. When something seems so purposeless, it can feel like the joke is on you. The Devil will make every effort to reach you, but it's crucial to press on—persevere!

God is aware of all the events taking place in your life. You are going through that season for a reason, and I can assure you it is for God's glory. You will eventually be content that those events occurred. But how can you endure the circumstance to understand God's purpose for you? It can only be done by holding onto hope.

Isaiah 40:31, which states, "Those who hope in the Lord will revive their strength, they will fly on wings like an eagle," passionately supports the need for hope. This verse also says those who hope in God will run without getting tired. This verse highlights the benefits of trusting the Lord during trying times.

God made each person uniquely, flawlessly flawed, and perfectly crowned for His glory. The good news is that a breakthrough occurs when the season becomes intolerable because you are no longer alone. As a loving Father, God will never allow you to face a season for which He has not given you the strength to endure.

Chapter 1

Horrific Moments Don't Last

Dear woman, you can only harness the energy of hope when times are tough, and you lose your strength. You'll be able to persevere if you have hope in the Lord during this time. Ironically, when we contrast our lives with those of others who appear to have it all together, we often find that they are dealing with the same or even worse problems. After the tests come tremendous gains.

> And he answered: Behold, I make a covenant before all your people; I will do wonders that have not been done in all the earth, nor any nation, and all the people in the midst of which you are will see the work of Jehovah; because what I will do with you will be a tremendous thing. (Exodus 34:10 KJV)

When we live in difficult seasons, the hand of God is seen differently. The book of Exodus shows us the nation of Israel, which suffered greatly from the confrontation with Pharaoh and had to go through the desert to reach the Promised Land. After that fight came a great victory. Israel's experiences demonstrate a lesson we must understand: a fight is a difficult season needed to conquer new lands.

The truth is that none of us wants to go through the desert or be chased by a pharaoh, but we all want to see new wonders. To see wonders, God has to put us against the sea to exercise our faith. If we want to see tremendous outcomes, we must persevere in difficult times and remember that God rewards us for our actions, not just our good intentions. Difficult moments provide the perfect space for us to focus on work that will cause God to perform incredibly.

"The Lord God will fight for you, and you will be calm. Then Jehovah said to Moses: Why do you cry to me? Tell the children of Israel to march" (Exodus 14:14-15 KJV).

The previous verse implies Moses wanted Israel to understand that in difficult moments, God walked with them so they could move forward calmly. He wanted them to see how God protected them. If we want to see how God extends the business, we have to advance in the business. The promise is that we will see wonders. If we want blessings in the ministry, we have to pray, fast, and evangelize. Then we will see wonders.

Most of us feel bad times will never end. But this is a subjective and erroneous perception of our minds. Do not hoard these negative thoughts. Dismiss them immediately because nothing lasts forever, not even the worst moments. "Tough times never last but tough people do (Robert H. Schuller).

When God tells us to relocate, He advances with us, saves us from danger, stretches us out, and takes us to a place where we will reach our prophetic goals.

As I said earlier, the tough times you are going through are so intense and difficult that you think they will last forever. But they will not. It just seems so.

You are heartbroken by disappointment. You feel the pain will not subside. But it will.

You live in a sea of doubt and see no signs of light on the horizon. That is what it seems like.

You work breaking your back, wondering if you will have to bear that heavy load forever. That is what it seems like.

You fail again and again. You cry and sink into frustration, resigned to history repeating itself. It seems as if it will.

The difficult days and nights are long for you in contrast to how fast the good times seemed to fly.

Dear woman, the discomfort takes up so much space that the happy moments are far away and blurred. It eclipses the good things in your life today, and you forget that this bad season will pass.

Everything is temporary: joys, sorrows, profits, and losses. You lived through happy moments. You lived through hard times.

Some experiences weakened you. Others made you stronger and wiser. But neither the current circumstances nor what you feel when life is turned upside down will last forever. It just seems so.

Do what you can to cope with this hard moment: cry, shout, reflect, talk to others, and sleep. Give the moment what it asks for.

Do what you have to do now and think no further.

Dear woman, affirm this prayer:

Dear God, we certainly want to walk by Your side, not only to see Your glory in the form of a cloud or a pillar of fire but also because we love and depend on You. Be our shield against the Enemy's attack. Our main direction to new lands and experiences is always rooted in You. Put in us the desire to stay close to Your heart so we can clearly understand where You want us to go, and how we will see Your glory in troublesome times. Amen.

Chapter 2

You Have Conquered Challenges Before

You have faced many difficulties throughout your life up until this point. You've overcome them in the past, and you will do so again. Maintain a positive attitude and cling to God. He is still alive to assist you now and always. He is the same yesterday, today, and tomorrow. He has helped you through previous difficulties.

Dry your tears. Claim your experience and all those good things that the discomfort has eclipsed. They are there with you. Whether you have more or fewer resources in your hands, can you take advantage of them?

Remember that this bad season will pass. You have the opportunity to focus on what you want to happen later. However, if you don't want to take advantage of it or don't feel strong enough, remember that with every second that passes, you are leaving this episode of your life. The bad times will pass. Now is the time to resume what can serve you from all you have experienced. And also how valuable you find it in these difficult times.

Perhaps you had days when you wanted to put on your pajamas, curl up in bed, and ask someone to wake you up when the trials were over. But dear woman or young girl, many wonderful things await you. In the days ahead, you will see the greatest manifestations of the Savior's power the world has ever seen. Until He returns "with power and great glory," He will bestow countless privileges, blessings, and miracles upon the faithful.

We certainly live in one of the most complicated times in the history of the world. The complexities cause many people to feel overwhelmed and exhausted.

Ruth followed her mother-in-law Naomi to Israel after the death of her husband where she met Boaz. They would eventually carry on the lineage of the Messiah and become King David's great-grandparents.

Ruth endured severe hardships because she was a woman in an ancient setting without protection. Ruth said, "Please don't push me to leave you or turn away from you. I will follow you everywhere you go and stay where you stay. My God will be your God, and your people, my people" (Ruth 1:16).

She courageously accompanied Naomi to the land of Israel and gave her life to the Lord. Her consistent faithfulness in the face of adversity made a significant contribution to God's victory over sin and death.

As seen in the story of Ruth, despite her tribulations and past, she conquered and moved on. Your past challenges are the manuals to conquer the present. Give tomorrow a chance. Let time show you that pain passes. Or, if it doesn't, it teaches you how to handle it.

Let me put before you love, joy, peace, and all the goodness that seems so far away today. Just because you're missing it right now doesn't mean you don't have the chance to feel it tomorrow. What does not happen today can happen tomorrow. What has not gone well for you today can be great tomorrow. What is not clear today, can be clear tomorrow.

You have verified that life flows, that it changes every day, and that you can decide to go in the direction you consider appropriate. Didn't it work today? Have you strayed today? Do you regret this day? Don't worry. Tomorrow will be different.

Chapter 3

God Is with You

One cannot emphasize enough that God is with us.

"God is our strength and refuge, a very near-by aid in times of need. Therefore, we won't be afraid even if the earth is removed and the mountains are dragged into the middle of the sea" (Psalm 46:1-2).

Regardless of the difficulties we face in life, He is always by our side.

Someone said, "Be nice to women. They constitute half of the population and are the mothers of the other half."

My dear sister, wonderful woman, who has chosen the best part, I greatly admire what you do. I see your hands in everything.

Maybe you are a mother, and that takes up all your time. You are a companion and the best friend your husband has had or will ever have. You are a housewife. That seems like a small thing. But what a job it is to keep a clean and tidy house. You are a buyer. Until quite late in life, I didn't realize what a demanding responsibility it is to ensure there is food in the pantry, clean and presentable clothes, and that everything necessary for the proper functioning of a household is bought.

You are a nurse. You are the first to be informed of any illness and the first to react and provide help. In serious illnesses, you are at the bedside of the sick day and night, comforting, encouraging, serving, and praying.

You are so many things to so many people; yet, you consider yourself a failure. You think that you cannot succeed and all your efforts will not be enough. We all have these feelings. I would like to encourage you, inspire you, thank you, compliment you, and bring you a little joy. I pray for that.

We all worry about whether we are succeeding. We would all like to do better. But unfortunately, we don't often see the results of what we do.

Despite the challenges and feelings of inadequacy, continue to do your best. Your efforts will benefit you and others. Don't dwell on a sense of failure. Kneel and ask the Lord to bless you. Put the matter in the hands of the Lord and then get up and do what is asked of you. You will find that you have accomplished something priceless. God is in the story. He is in the details.

"All who call on the Lord in truth will find him close by" (Psalm 145:18).

Some Christians worry that God will abandon them. I have experienced that feeling a lot in my life because many teachers misled me as a child, telling me that if I made a mistake even once, God would forsake me. But this verse serves as a reminder that those who call on God will hear from Him. We can be confident that God will never leave us, even in our darkest hours when we feel He has abandoned us to the wolves. He is present even when we cannot trace Him.

Be strong, bold, and courageous! Move forward with joy in your eyes and love in your heart. How blessed you are, dear mother! You have children who will be yours forever. I hope you have been sealed in the house of the Lord and that your family will be eternal in the kingdom of our Father.

"Look, I'm knocking at the door. I will enter and eat with him if he hears my voice and opens the door, and he will join me" (Revelation 3:20).

Perhaps, like me, you had some teachers who gave you the false idea that you had to get your life together before you could approach God. No. God approaches us. He knocks at the door. The passage indicates that we must open it, but God doesn't wait for us to have squeaky-clean lives.

God is with us. These four little words can change lives. Many of us have had friends or family members forsake us, but we have God, a solid foundation, who will never turn His back on us. Take comfort in these words.

Count your blessings one by one. What you need is a comfortable and pleasant home where love dwells. Someone said there is no finer picture than a good woman who cooks for the people she loves. Carefully evaluate what you are doing.

May you receive strength to carry your heavy load, meet all your obligations, walk alongside a good, faithful, and loving man, and bring up your children in righteousness and truth with him. Nothing you possess, no secular good you acquire, will be so valuable as the love of your children. God bless you, dear sister and mother.

Chapter 4

It Is a Learning Phase

A common belief in personal development is that failure is inadequate feedback. We frequently overlook this when experiencing trying times in our lives. We view failure as a sign that we are ineffective or off-course.

Dear woman, most of life's learning occurs through trial and error. The sensible course of action when things don't go your way is to try to figure out why and take something away from the experience. Using the lessons you've learned from that experience, you'll eventually be able to turn things around.

Human beings live immersed in a constant process of personal change. As the years go by and we live new experiences, personal changes allow us to grow, get to know each other, adapt, and live with well-being. However, those personal changes sometimes get stuck.

When we encounter unpleasant experiences such as breakups, crises within relationships, fear of uncertainty, insecurity, etc., we live with constant blocks that make us repeat the same experiences and situations.

The key is to engage in a process of personal change that makes you more aware of what is happening to you, how you manage it, and how you could manage it differently to grow.

We cannot control the world, people, or what happens. But we can learn to understand ourselves and, from our transformation, we can make everything change. It does not mean that we are to blame for what is happening. Rather, the only and most valuable thing you can do is focus on your change, not on what is happening outside.

Are you excited and determined? Are you going to cry, or will you roll up your sleeves and get to work?

"I consider that our present hardships are not worth relating with the glory that will be conveyed in us" (Romans 8:18).

The world has a few sayings similar to Romans 8:18 such as "Good things come to those who wait." However, Romans 8:18 is about 1000 times better because it goes much deeper than that sentiment. What we experience here on Earth, be it good or bad, cannot possibly be compared to the kingdom of God that is to come.

You take on a victim mentality when obstacles arise, and I think I may know why this happens. In hard times, we feel as if the universe is messing with us. But it's the opposite! You are in the learning phase.

Why not change your thinking and perceive the obstacles as a personal challenge? Instead of thinking the universe is messing with you, think of it as challenging you to find a solution.

Dear woman, say to yourself, "Okay, that's the way it happened; now, what will I do about it?" Put your skills to work to achieve the solution to the problem.

Once we start to change our attitude toward obstacles and challenges, overcoming them may even become fun. Our competitive human nature rises and prepares us to win in all our endeavors. We develop a steely determination not to be hit with discouragement.

Chapter 5

It Happens to Everyone

We occasionally succumb to the cunning trick our minds play on us in difficult times. They try to make us believe we are the only ones going through this. But after some thought, you'll see we all face unique challenges. You're less aware of other people's problems because you're too focused on your own; they're unique to you. This gives the impression that other people's lives are much smoother than yours. But the reality is whatever happens to you also happens to nearly everyone else—if not worse.

We are always in the middle of any phase we are going through in life. Challenges are universal. They are not restricted to you alone. If only human intestines were transparent like a mirror, we would see what others are going through.

Life is complete with challenges. Some people satisfy every undertaking with self-belief, while others battle to triumph over them. Your maximum self wishes you to research and grow.

The trouble is that every too often, you might confront identical demanding situations repeatedly. That's when you start to lose motivation to stand against the issue, and you lose sight of the possible lesson. Challenges can emerge and spiral you into despair and frustration.

"For whoever is born of God conquers the world, and our faith is the success that has to conquer the world" (1 John 5:4).

Woman, you are born of God and have His life, *Zoe*, in you; you can overcome every obstacle.

As a co-author of your reality, you can conquer these challenges. With this sense of obligation and cognizance, you can start your journey to a better nation where challenges are no longer demanding situations but opportunities to glimpse your maximum self.

Here are some ways to better meet whatever challenges you may face.

Face the Project
In many cases, this is the most critical and obvious step, but it is also the one most often missed. As humans, we spend time trying to find out why the problem occurred or wallow in self-pity at how enormous the situation is. Even ordinary things like a pileup of laundry or work go unnoticed. Putting off a project doesn't make it depart. This applies to big demanding situations and small ones. The most vital thing you can do is face what's in front of you head-on.

Be Present

Do not undervalue the power of being a gift, dear woman. You will discover that most challenges are not challenges at all. Make it a habit to face challenges—even in failure—with full presence and cognizance. Meditation will let you cultivate silent focus and is a great practice to help bring consciousness to yourself during tough times.

You may ask yourself questions to help you better apprehend the trouble and how it impacts you.

- Why is this a mission?
- Do I accept as true that I'm capable of being a success in this venture?
- What are the viable effects if I prevail?
- What's the outcome if I fail?

Those questions aren't intended to remedy the problem; as an alternative, they may be intended to convey to you a fuller consciousness of the venture itself and your emotional reaction to it.

Check Yourself for the Answer

Others can help you arrive at your very own know-how. However, no one ever solves your troubles. Even in situations where someone else is appearing as an expert or associate, most effectively, you can determine for yourself how you should solve the problem. The longer you spend trying to avoid the situation, the longer the situation will remain. Assess the scenario, your assets, and your abilities, and then act. Your actions may encompass enlisting help from others, but it'll be your project to solve. The sooner you take up the mission, the quicker it stops being a problem.

Understand Yourself

Challenges present opportunities for growth. That increase takes place out of your potentiality, which is limitless and exceedingly active in each moment of life. Come to recognize yourself as that. Demanding situations are spikes in that imaginary, difficult barrier that guide you to recognition. You decide: Are you constrained, or are you an ever-expansive increase of awareness and love? Choose the latter and examine that so-known venture you've been going through.

There is a reason why positive, demanding situations seem difficult to you, even as others breeze right through the equal conditions. It's not that they are better than you. It's about perspective. Those who face difficulties have discovered ways to avoid seeing them as insurmountable.

Detach from the Outcome

Stop stressing about the final results. When you do this, you end up making a mountain out of a molehill. Once you shift your attention to the issue you're truly encountering, as opposed to the result, the most intimidating elements of your trials disappear. If you carry out the mission without worrying about the outcome, you have power over the state of affairs.

Some problems appear to be huge and vicious, but if you maintain your focus and awareness on the right things, no venture is too large to meet with strength and style.

"Because I, the Lord your God, will hold your right hand and encourage you, "Fear not; I will help you" (Isaiah 41:13).

Believe God when He tells you not to be afraid. Of course, you need faith to believe Him. Remember what faith means. According to Hebrews 11:1, faith is "evidence for things unseen, the substance of things hoped for."

God is present even though you cannot see or touch Him. I glance out the window whenever I need a reminder. How can you not believe it when you look at the flowers, trees, mountains, lakes, and streams? All of them were made by God.

Chapter 6

There's Always Something to Be Grateful For

The fact that some aspects of your life aren't going well is less than ideal. But if you think about it, many things are going well. Your career is still on track, even if your family is not doing well. Even though the difficult seasons may break you, if you take the time to evaluate the positive aspects of your life, you will have greater expectations of better days ahead.

"Be joyful always, pray constantly, and show gratitude in all circumstances; God expects this of you for you to be united to Christ Jesus" (1 Thessalonians 5:16–18).

The above verse encourages us to always thank God because that is what He wants. By doing His will, He will give you the joy you deserve.

Everyone has a different situation, and the details of each life are unique. Nevertheless, I learned that there is one thing that removes the sourness that can enter our lives. We can do something to make life happier and even more beautiful. We can be grateful!

It may seem contrary to the world's wisdom to suggest that someone overwhelmed with grief should give thanks to God. But people who put aside the bottle of sourness and, instead, lift the cup of gratitude, can find a purifying drink that cures and gives peace and understanding.

Why does the Lord command us to be grateful?

All of these commandments are given to enable us to access blessings. The commandments are opportunities to exercise our agency and receive blessings. Our loving heavenly Father knows that if we choose to cultivate a spirit of gratitude, it will bring us joy and great happiness. Be grateful for something. But some may say, "What can I be grateful for when my universe collapses?"

We may be applying the wrong method when we focus on the things we are grateful for. It is difficult to cultivate a grateful mind if gratitude is only proportional to the number of blessings we can count. While it is important to count our blessings frequently, and anyone who has tried to do so knows that they are many, I do not believe the Lord expects us to be less grateful in times of trial than in times of abundance and calm. Most scriptural references do not speak of thankfulness for things but suggest a general spirit or attitude of gratitude.

"I will honor the name of the Lord Most High and give thanks to the Lord for his righteousness" (Psalm 7:17).

It's easy to be grateful for things when life is going the way we want. But what about the times when what we want seems so out of reach?

I propose we consider gratitude a state of mind, a way of living independent of our current situation. In other words, I propose that instead of being "thankful for things," we be "thankful for our situation," whatever it is.

We can decide to be grateful, no matter what.

This kind of recognition transcends everything that happens around us. It overcomes disappointment, discouragement, and despair. It blooms just as beautifully in icy winter landscapes as it does in the pleasant warmth of summer.

When we are grateful to God for our situation, we can experience sweet peace amid tribulation. In pain, we still manage to lift our hearts in praise. In suffering, we can give glory to the atonement of Christ. In the coldness of deep sorrow, we can feel close to heaven and the warmth of heaven's embrace.

Sometimes we think that being grateful is what we do after our issues are solved, but that is petty. We lose a lot when we wait for the rainbow to thank God for the rain.

Being grateful in times of sadness does not mean we are happy with our situation. It means that through the eyes of faith, we look beyond our present difficulties.

This is not recognition expressed in words but recognition from the soul. It is gratitude that heals the heart and expands the mind.

Gratitude Is an Act of Faith

Being grateful in our situation is an act of faith in God. It requires that we trust in God and hope for things we do not see but are true. In being grateful, we follow the example of our beloved Savior, who said, "Not my will, but yours be done."

True gratitude is the expression of hope and testimony. It comes from acknowledging that we don't always understand life's trials, but we trust that one day, we will have that understanding.

> Do not worry about anything; instead, bring your requests to God in every circumstance through prayer and petition, along with thanksgiving. And in Christ Jesus, the peace of God, which passes all comprehension, will guard your hearts and minds. (Philippians 4:6-7)

In all circumstances, our sense of gratitude is nourished by the many sacred truths we know to be true: that our Father has given His children the great plan of prosperity, through the atonement of Jesus Christ, we can live forever with our loved ones. In the end, we will have glorious, perfect, and immortal bodies, free from disease or handicap, and an abundance of happiness and joy will replace our tears of sadness and grief.

It must have been this kind of testimony that transformed the Savior's apostles, turning them from fearful and uncertain men into bold and joyful emissaries of the Master. In the hours following the crucifixion, they were consumed with despair and grief, unable to comprehend what had just happened. But one event changed everything. Their Lord appeared to them and said to them, "See My hands and My feet; it is I."

When the apostles recognized the risen Christ and experienced the glorious resurrection of their beloved Savior, they became different men. Nothing could stop them from accomplishing their mission. They accepted the torture, humiliation, and even death they would have to suffer for their testimonies with courage and determination. Nothing could stop them from praising and serving their Lord. They changed the lives of people everywhere. They changed the world.

You don't have to see the Savior as the apostles did to encounter the same transformation. Your testimony of Christ, given by the Holy Ghost, can help you look beyond the sad endings of mortality and see the bright future the Redeemer of the world has prepared.

CONCLUSION

In conclusion, it is better to draw strength from the Spirit by praying to God during any trying time you find yourself in, than feel depressed and brooding. Although it may be challenging, it will be beneficial to set aside your emotional ties to the issue and let God take the reins. God will never abandon you to suffer because He loves you. He will always be there for you in love.

A new season will start after this one concludes. And you'll be astounded by your accomplishments when you reflect on the success of the season you've just finished. Please remember that even when it seems as if God is tearing you apart, He is strengthening you. Maintain your attention. Rest assured! You will be blessed with courage; wisdom will adorn you, and victory is already yours.

Martin Luther King Jr. said, "We must accept infinite disappointment but never lose infinite hope." Keep this advice in mind whenever you feel like giving up. Hold these words close to your heart for those times when you feel there is no reason to continue. Always remember you are a strong, beautiful, energetic woman who can withstand any storm.

Finally, apostle James advises his readers to

Count it all joy, my brothers and sisters, when various trials arise, for you know that the fruit of your faith working in such adversity is endurance. So that you can be flawless and complete, lacking nothing, make sure your endurance carries you the entire way without failing. (James 1:2 Good News)

"My brethren, count it all joy" as the KJV says! In every situation, let's believe that hope is a rainbow.

About The Author

Je Taun Barron is a woman with a story of pain, loss, and hope. After losing her father, she faced the hardest moments of her life, and turned to her faith in God to see her through. But her hope wavered and she asked God painful questions. Growing up, she'd been close to her father, and her heart shattered when she lost him. But when he visited her in a dream, he told her not to be sad and never to lose hope. A message that has carried her through - a message she hopes can help others through their own darkest days and harshest trials.

Je Taun is a wife and mother of three beautiful children. She enjoys cooking, writing, and advocating for body positivity for women and girls. She hopes to encourage, motivate, and inspire as many people as possible and is the Founder of Perfectly Imperfect Foundation, which promotes positive body image, self-love, and self-esteem for women and girls. She wants to encourage women and girls to know that they are beautiful, valuable, and loved by God. After all, God can heal our hearts, renew our souls, and see us through anything... if we allow His grace to shine on our lives.

For more information visit her website
www.JetaunBarron.com

www.ingramcontent.com/pod-product-compliance
Lightning Source LLC
Chambersburg PA
CBHW051602120626
46551CB00013B/1633